BYGONE WOKIN

BYGONE
WOKING

Iain Wakeford

Phillimore

1983

Published by
PHILLIMORE & CO. LTD.
Shopwyke Hall, Chichester, Sussex

ISBN 0 85033 506 X

Printed and bound in Great Britain by
BILLING & SONS LTD
Worcester, England

LIST OF ILLUSTRATIONS

ACKNOWLEDGEMENTS

I would like to thank everybody who has lent me photographs for the book and project: Mrs. Boarer, Mr. N. Brackley, Mr. D. Chapman, Mr. J. Clarke, Miss M. Cooper, Mrs. E. Cuttle, Mr. T. Fuller, Mrs. G. Garforth, Mr. T. Harding, Mr. J. Hay, Mr. P. Kangis, Mr. C. Mileham, Mrs. M. Smith (all members of the Mayford and Woking District History Society), Mr. Backhouse, Mr. R. Bowers, Mr. H. Boxall, Mr. N. Burnett, Mrs. K. Coveney, Mr. J. Dall, Mr. K. Durrant, Mr. B. Elkins, Mr. C. Elton, Mr. S. Fox, Mrs. Gay, Mr. K. Halls, Mr. F. Herd, Mrs. J. Jackman, Mr. R. Jones, Miss J. Ledger, Mr. Pring, Mrs. J. Roles and Mr. T. Rozelaar. Mr. H. Bayliss and Mr. M. Shawcross have also kindly provided information for the captions.

I would also like to thank the Mayford and Woking District History Society for allowing me to use their collection of old photographs, as well as the Surrey Fire Brigade, Unwin Brothers Ltd. and especially the Woking Borough Council (Mr. Borrell, Mr. Mathews and Mr. Shipp).

Whilst it would not have been possible to have compiled this book without the help of those mentioned above, it would also have been impossible for me to complete this task without the help and encouragement of my parents and my brother, Neil. I am most grateful for their comments on the text and for their help in typing and checking the captions.

INTRODUCTION

This book is one of the results of a project that I started a few years ago for the Mayford and Woking District History Society, called Woking's Pictorial Past. The aim of the project is to gather together, preserve, and make available to the general public any photograph of anywhere within the borough of Woking, that for one reason or another cannot be taken again.

This book deals with the period up to the early 1930s. It shows Woking as it looked over half a century ago, long before the modern town centre was built. For older residents of the area it will, no doubt, bring back many memories, whilst for the visitor and younger inhabitants I hope it will show that Woking does have a history, despite popular belief to the contrary. If you are unfamiliar with the area and its history, I hope that the following will help you understand the district's development up to and including the period covered by this book.

Evidence of prehistoric man's existence has been found in almost every district within the borough of Woking. Stone Age flints, Bronze Age burial mounds, Iron Age axe heads, and Romano-British pottery, all show that this area has been inhabited for thousands of years. Early documents record several places within the borough, such as Pyrford (959 A.D.), Woking (708-715) and Byfleet (727). These three also appear in the Domesday Book (1086) where Sutton is also mentioned. The ancient parish churches of St Peter's (Old Woking) and St Nicholas' (Pyrford) both date from Norman times, whilst Byfleet and Horsell (both dedicated to St Mary) were begun during the 14th century.

The manors of Woking, Pyrford, Byfleet and Sutton all passed into and out of royal hands, whilst the smaller manors and sub-manors such as Horsell, Woodham, Crastock (Mayford), Hollands (Goldsworth) and Townesley (Pyrford) were controlled by local farmers or the larger manors. The area was mainly agricultural: up to the mid-19th century over 60 per cent of the workforce were employed on the land. In Pyrford the figure was over 90 per cent and even in Woking, where there was a small amount of industry, nearly 50 per cent were still working on local farms or nurseries.

The villages were small, sometimes clustered around a village green as at Kingfield, Westfield, Mayford and Sutton Green, or along a main road, like Woking and Byfleet. Pyrford and Horsell had no village centre, and areas such as Knaphill and Maybury were merely squatter settlements on the edge of the vast Woking common. It was this common (which stretched from Brookwood to Byfleet) that was to help change the appearance of the Woking area during the late 19th century.

Because commonland was cheap, both the Basingstoke canal (1793) and the London and South Western Railway (1838) were constructed over Woking's heath. The London and South Western Railway Co. also built a station at Woking, and in 1840 the *Railway Hotel* was built nearby. However, whilst the land was cheap, the train fare to London was not, and as there was still plenty of undeveloped land nearer to the capital, no town grew up beside Woking station.

By the 1850s London's graveyards were becoming overcrowded. In 1851 the London Necropolis and National Mausoleum Co. was formed. They received parliamentary permission to buy over 2,300 acres of Woking common upon which they planned to build a massive cemetery. The cheap land, sandy soil and remoteness from habitation made the common an ideal place for a cemetery, whilst the railway meant that the centre of London was still less than an hour away. Only 400 acres were actually laid out—the present Brookwood Cemetery. Trees were planted, and a railway line was constructed with two stations. This enabled funeral parties from London to travel by rail to the cemetery.

In 1855 the Necropolis Co. sought permission to sell some of their land, and in 1858 the Home Office bought 67 acres at Knaphill for a prison. In 1860, 150 acres were acquired for an asylum, and a further 10 acres were sold to the Royal Dramatic College at Maybury. The profits from these sales, together with statements made when the company was formed, led some people to believe that the Necropolis Co. were in fact 'a building society masquerading as a burial company'. Others, however, have pointed out that all the 2,300 acres may well have been intended for cemetery use; when the Necropolis Co. was set up the practice of cremation had not been introduced, and there were serious proposals to close all the graveyards in London. Whatever the reason, the fact is that the Necropolis Co. now had the chance to sell portions of Woking commonland. However, despite making vast profits from the institutions, the sale of land around Woking station was not a success. By the mid-1860s there was still no sign of a town at Woking, although by now another hotel (the *Albion*) had been built.

In 1864 and 1869 the Necropolis Co. sought, and received, Parliament's permission to sell all but 560 acres of their land. The way was now clear for a town to be built. The most likely position for the town seemed to be to the south of the station towards Woking village, but for one reason or another this did not occur. For a long time the Rastrick family were held responsible for the town being built on the 'wrong side' of the railway. They owned the piece of land immediately to the south of the station and refused to sell. However, recent evidence has shown that development could still have taken place, and that the Necropolis Co. were to blame. They divided their land to the south into large expensive plots, to encourage high class residential development, whilst the land on the north was sold in smaller plots, intended for commercial and low-class dwellings.

In 1870 a row of newly-constructed houses in the High Street were converted into shops. Soon purpose-built premises were being erected, mainly in the High Street, Broadway, Chertsey and Chobham Roads, although other shops were later built along Commercial Road, Guildford Road and Goldsworth Road. Schools, churches and hospitals were also constructed. A school was built in 1875 by the Woking School Board (in Board School Road). A Methodist chapel was built in 1872 (in Chapel Street) and the Church of England had a corrugated iron church for worship in Providence Street (later renamed Church Street). This building was later replaced by Christ Church. The first hospital in Woking was in Bath Road, where the Woking, Horsell and Woodham Cottage Hospital opened in 1893. Six years later the Victoria Cottage Hospital was opened in Chobham Road, next to Wheatsheaf Bridge.

Gradually over the years, the services of the town grew as the population increased. The largest growth in the area was during the 1890s, when Heathside, Maybury and Hook Heath were being developed. The increase in housing caused many problems. When Woking Urban District Council was formed in 1895, there were only three made-up roads in the area; from Guildford to Chertsey via Woking town or Maybury, and the road through Goldsworth to Knaphill; the rest were mere tracks. It was the provision of a sewerage system for the town that was the main concern of the Council. In 1894 the Local Board (the predecessor of the U.D.C.) decided on a scheme whereby the sewage would be pumped to a site at Scotcher's Farm, Horsell. When the W.U.D.C. came into office, however, they rejected this plan in favour of a sewage works off Carters Lane, Old Woking. Work began in 1896 and was completed at a total cost of £64,000 in 1899.

Another concern for the W.U.D.C. was the condition of the bridges over the Basingstoke Canal. They had been constructed during the 1790s, and by the turn of the century were in desperate need of repair. The council demolished the old arches, and eventually constructed new bridges that could cope with the increased traffic of the 20th century. The widening of Victoria Arch (named in 1898), Triggs Lane and Hermitage Hill were also carried out by the Council during this period. In less than fifty years Woking had been transformed from an open heath into a thriving town with shops, offices, hospital, churches and schools. With an excellent train service to London, and plenty of land for development it is not surprising that Woking soon became the largest town in Surrey.

Of course, the development of Woking soon had an effect on the surrounding villages. During the 1890s many of the small farms and nurseries of Horsell were sold and their land developed. In Knaphill and St John's, the building of the convict prison and lunatic asylum were responsible for growth. (The prison was later converted by the War Department into Inkerman Barracks.) St John's was also chosen as the site for the first crematorium in Britain. It was built by the Cremation Society of England in 1879, but was not used until 1885 as the law regarding cremation was uncertain. At Brookwood, it was the opening of the main line railway station in 1868 which led to the village being built. Sutton Green and Mayford appear to have escaped widespread development during this period, and even in Old Woking the effects of the nearby town were not felt until after the First World War, when the area to the north of the main street was developed.

Pyrford was not affected by the growth of Woking. On its northern border, however, some development did take place. In 1887 a station was opened at Byfleet Corner to serve the communities of Pyrford, Byfleet and Woodham (the station later became known as West Byfleet). As a result a new community grew up on the commonland of Byfleet, just as the town of Woking had done on Woking common. The village of Byfleet became famous in 1907 for the motor track of Brooklands built by Mr H. F. Locke-King. An airfield was also provided, and during the First World War the area became the centre of aircraft production in this country. This continued after the war, bringing employment and growth to the village.

The story of Woking and its surrounding districts is a story of constant change. Unfortunately we cannot see what the area was like before the railway came. We are lucky, however, that some of the later changes have been captured on film, so that we can now at least see Woking's development from the 1880s right up to the present day.

FURTHER READING

The Borough of Woking

Crosby, A., *A History of Woking.*

Woking

Amos, F. R., *The Origins of Christ Church, Woking, A Short History.*
Greenwood, G. B., *Woking & District, A Dictionary of Local History.*
Locke, A., *Woking Past.*
Whiteman, J. R. and S. E., *Victorian Woking*

Pyrford

Lewin, S., *A Short History of Pyrford and Wisley.*
Lewin, S., *St Nicholas, Pyrford, A Guide and Short History.*

Byfleet

Stevens, L. R., *Byfleet, A Village in England.*
Stevens, L. R., *The Church of St Mary the Virgin, Byfleet.*

Brookwood

Clarke, J., *The Brookwood Necropolis Railway*

Sutton Green

Albion, G., *St Edward's, Sutton Green.*

The Mayford & Woking District History Society publish a bi-monthly newsletter full of information on various aspects of local history. They have also produced several leaflets on a number of local topics. The Surrey & Hampshire Canal Society have a number of books on the history etc. of the Basingstoke Canal with reference to places in Woking. The Horsell Common Preservation Society have produced a book of four walks on Horsell Common with a short introduction to its history.

All these books, and many more, are available in the local history reference section of Woking Central Library.

1. Woking Railway Station, c. 1900, with the shops of the High Street, the old signal box and the workmen's huts on the right. On the platform to the left can be seen milk churns awaiting collection. The original station on Woking Common, built in 1838, consisted of a small two-storey building, with two platforms connected by a bridge.

2. Woking Station. Ashbys Bank, on the corner of Chertsey Road and the Broadway, can be seen just to the left of the canopy. The milk churns can still be seen on the platform. The station was rebuilt in 1883 when the number of lines was increased, the platforms were lengthened and the bridge was replaced by a subway. The present station was built in 1936.

Woking Station

3. The Woking and District Bus Service, outside the North entrance of Woking Railway Station, c. 1921. Mr J.R. Fox started the Woking and District Bus Service in 1921 with a converted model 'T' Ford carrying passengers from Woking Station to St John's. His son Mr S. Fox can be seen here, standing beside this first bus.

4. F.W. Renshaws – 'The Grey Bus Service' – outside the North entrance of Woking Station, c. 1922. The Grey bus service run by Renshaws of St. John's operated during the early 1920s, between Woking Station, St. John's, Horsell and Knaphill. They also drove a converted model 'T' Ford, which had been extended to carry more passengers.

5. A.G. Smith Bus Service — The Broadway, Woking. In addition to Mr Fox and Mr Renshaw, Mr A.G. Smith also operated a bus service, between Woking and Knaphill.

Maybury Road, Woking.

6. Maybury Road, c. 1916. The three bus companies already mentioned, together with many other small firms in the district, gave Woking an excellent bus service in the early years of this century. They all picked up passengers from Woking Station, stopping, as they do today, along the Broadway.

7. Courtney Road, c. 1905, near the corner of North Road and the beginning of Board School Road. Council work-men are seen here laying a concrete pipe across Courtney Road from the Electric Light Works towards the Basingstoke Canal and the offices of the Gas Company.

8. Spanton's Timber Yard, 1927, with the houses of Boundary Road and the Gas Works in the background. The canal had begun to decline in the early part of this century, when the lock gates near St John's were damaged. From then on trade was restricted to the lower reaches, as far as Arthur's Bridge. The main cargo was coal for the gas works and timber for the yards of Brewster's and Spanton's.

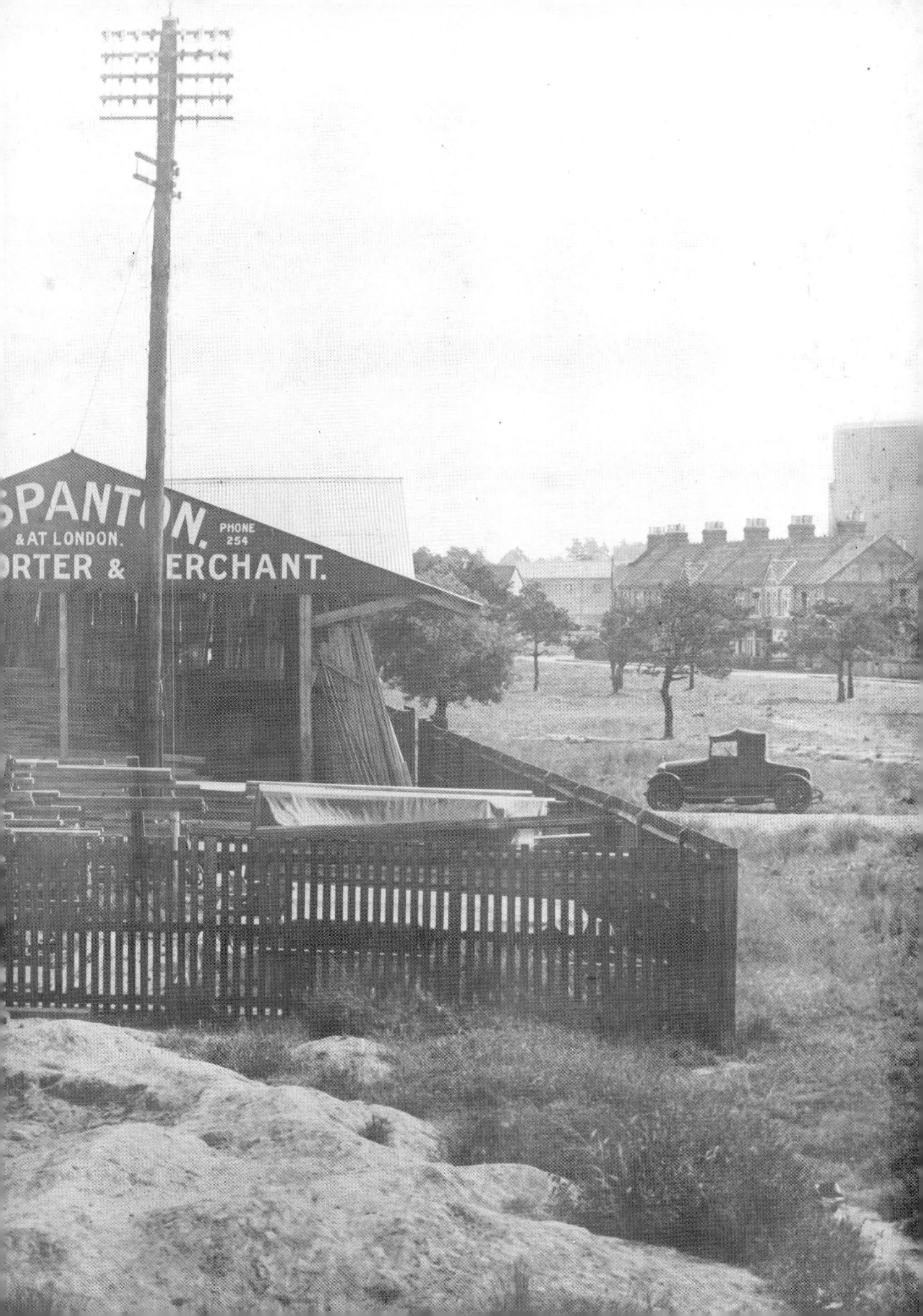
SPANTON.
& AT LONDON.
PHONE
254
ORTER & ERCHANT.

9.   Chertsey Road Bridge, c. 1905. The original Chertsey Road Bridge crossed the canal at right angles. It was very narrow and the scene of many accidents in the early days of motoring. It was built in the 1790s for horse-drawn traffic and by 1906 it was so badly damaged that the Urban District Council were forced to carry out repairs.

10.   Chertsey Road Bridge, 1922, taken from the Maybury side of the bridge. In 1907 the Council demolished the old arch and constructed a temporary wooden bridge. They then took the owners of the Canal to court in an attempt to get them to pay for the repairs. The complex court case that followed resulted in the canal company's favour, and the W.U.D.C. were forced to pay for the reconstruction of all canal bridges in Woking. The present bridge was built in 1923.

1. Chertsey Road, from the top of the old bridge looking out over Boundary Road Common towards the town centre. Brook House and the Victoria Way roundabout would dominate the centre of this picture today.

2. Chertsey Road, c. 1900, with the corner of Board School Road, which gets its name from the school that was built here in 1874. On the left can be seen the grocery shop of W. Everson. All the buildings in this picture have been pulled down with the exception of those, just visible, nearest the station.

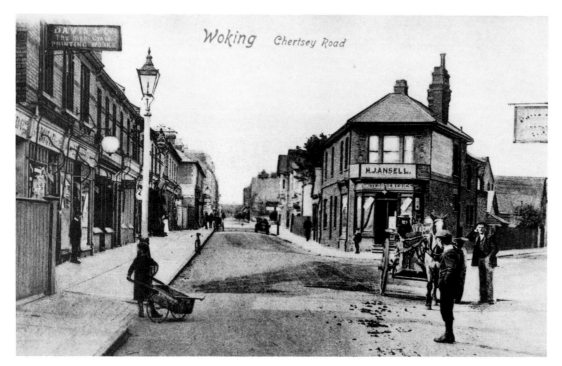

13.　Chertsey Road, and the corner of Church Street, looking towards Woking Station. On the corner are the premises of H.J. Ansell, grocer and beer retailer. Davis and Company, the printing works, is on the left.

14.　Chertsey Road, at the corner of Commercial Road and Walton Road. On the right along Commercial Road can be seen the sign of Bond's Dining Rooms and Temperance Hotel. Further down this road can be seen the Woking Drug Store. The large removal van belongs to Robertson Brothers of North Road, Woking.

15. Chertsey Road, looking from the corner of Chobham Road towards G.S. Addisons, the tobacconists, on the corner of Addison Road. Next door is Pearks Stores with a sign saying 'Offices To Let' on the first floor. W.E. Mallard, the tailors, and R. Wasleys, the butchers, occupy the next two shops. The yard of the old Red House Hotel is on the left.

16. F. Pullinger, 10 Chertsey Road, c. 1904.
F. Pullinger, pastrycook & baker, set up shop in Woking in 1883. This advertisement card, sent in December 1904, gives some idea of the goods he sold — 'Home-made Christmas puddings and mincemeat, iced Christmas cakes, bonbons, crackers and novelties', with 'Peter's, Caillers, and Cadbury's chocolates in great variety.'

17.   Chertsey Road. Opposite Pullinger's shop was the Post Office, built in 1895. Before 1865 all the mail for Woking was distributed from Ripley. After that date, letters and parcels arrived by rail to be sorted at Woking.

18.   Ashby's Bank, with the original Woking Urban District Council offices above. Since the formation of the Fire Brigade in 1895 the Council had been urged to provide a steam powered engine. They refused because of the cost, but at the same time they were prepared to spend £6,000 on new Council offices in Commercial Road. The long running dispute that followed resulted in several councillors being defeated in the local elections of 1898. The new council ordered an engine, but before it arrived the council offices above Ashby's Bank were burnt out on the 6th June 1899. The bank and a caretaker's room on the same floor were undamaged.

Woking. Chertsey Road.

19.   The Albion Hotel was one of Woking's best known buildings. The original hotel was built in 1856-57 by Reuben Percy. In 1899 it was demolished and a new hotel was built soon after. This too disappeared during the 1960s when the present complex was built.

20.   Chobham Road, on the corner of Commercial Road. This view of Chobham Road at the turn of the century would be unrecognisable today. The Woking Drug Stores on the right later became Wearing's and is now replaced with the shops below the Crown Life building. J.F. Gammon's is just visible on the left. The British Home Stores now occupies this site.

PHOTO. BY GARLANDS' STUDIO.   PRINTED AND PUBLISHED BY DAVIS & CO., WOKING.

CHOBHAM ROAD.

21. Chobham Road, c. 1909. Compare this to the previous picture and it will be seen that the vacant site next to Wearing's has been replaced by a motor garage and the shop of Skeet & Jeffes. Mr Skeet started business in Woking in 1891, and joined company with Mr Jeffes in 1901.

22. Chobham Road, Woking, looking towards Wheatsheaf Bridge. On the right can be seen the Victoria Cottage Hospital and the garden wall of Riverside House. This house later became an annexe to the Hospital, but has since been demolished to make way for Woking's by-pass (Victoria Way).

23. The Old Wheatsheaf Bridge and the Victoria Hospital. The Cottage Hospital, opened in 1899, was built to commemorate the Diamond Jubilee of Queen Victoria.

24. Wheatsheaf Bridge. The original Wheatsheaf Bridge was only 11 ft. wide. It was demolished in 1913, when the bridge seen in this picture was constructed.

Woking. Christchurch.

25.   Christ Church, c. 1904. This picture was taken before the church was completed.
Because of financial problems, the construction took over twenty years, from the laying of
the foundation stone by the Duchess of Albany in 1887, to its completion in 1908. Christ
Church parish was formed in 1893.

26.   Christ Church, c. 1932. The first vicar of Christ Church was the Rev. W.F.T. Hamilton, who, as the vicar of St John
had helped raise most of the money for the construction of Christ Church. It was he who bought the land on which the o
church hall was constructed in 1898. The chimney of the Electric Light Company can be seen in the distance along with
the shops and houses of Church Street and Chobham Road.

CHRIST CHURCH, CHURCH ROAD, WOKING.

7.   The Central Fire Station, c. 1914. The original Woking Fire Station was in a small corrugated iron shed in
hertsey Road. There were only eight members, with a further twelve volunteers divided equally amongst stations at
naphill, St John's and Woking village. This picture shows the second Central Fire Station, which was built at the rear
f the Urban District Council offices in Commercial Road.

28.   The Woking Fire Station, Church Street, c. 1932.   The fire that destroyed the Urban
District Council offices above Ashby's Bank in 1899 resulted in the Fire Brigade being granted
their request for assistance. In 1919 a motor engine with a telescopic ladder was purchased
from Dennis Brothers of Guildford. In 1925 a second engine was bought and in the same
year a Renault car donated by Councillor Illingsworth was converted as a motor tender.
On 21 July 1928 the Brigade moved into new premises built for £4,900 in Church Street.
This building was replaced by the present Fire Station in 1981.

29. Commercial Road, c. 1905. The row of buildings opposite Victoria Arch were perhaps the best known in Woking. This picture was taken before the council offices were erected on the site between the Public Halls, on the left, and the Constitutional Club.

30. Council Offices, Commercial Road. Plans for a building on this site costing £6,000 were abandoned in 1898. This building, costing £4,500, was finally approved and erected in 1905.

32. *(opposite page)* Interior of Wesleyan Church, Commercial Road, c. 1906. Woking's first Wesleyan Church was built in Chapel Street in 1872. This was enlarged during 1884 and the main entrance changed from Chapel Street to Commercial Road. It became the public library in March 1929. In January 1905 the church moved along Commercial Road to a site adjacent to the Constitutional Club.

PUBLIC BUILDINGS & WESLEYAN CHAPEL, WOKING.

31.   Commercial Road. From left to right can be seen the Woking Water Company offices, the Woking Public Halls, the U.D.C. offices, the Constitutional Club and the Wesleyan Church. The water company was formed in 1881 to supply the area with piped water from a reservoir at Clandon. The Grand Theatre was built in 1895 and the Constitutional Club was erected in 1898. All these buildings were demolished and were replaced by Maples, the Post Office and Cawsey Way.

The Wesleyan Church. Woking.

Published at Elton's Library.

Wesleyan Church & Public Buildings, Woking.

33.   Sparrow Park, c. 1908.
Victoria Gardens on the corner of
Commercial Road and the High Street
was planted in 1904 in memory of Queen
Victoria. These gardens were known
locally as Sparrow Park. This picture was
taken from the railway embankment.

35.   High Street, Woking, looking towards
Woking Station from the corner of Chapel
Street. In the 1870s a row of houses
which had recently been erected along
the High Street were converted into
shops. This was the beginning of Woking
as a shopping centre.

PEACE CELEBRATIONS at WOKING 20

34. Peace Celebrations, 1919.
When the Great War ended in 1918,
Woking, like many other towns and
villages throughout the country, wanted
to remember the dead and celebrate
peace. This picture of Commercial Road
shows part of the long procession that
wound its way through the streets of
Woking. Banners on the Public Halls and
Council Offices read: 'We Fought for
Humanity & Won', and 'God Save the
King, Long May Peace Continue'.

36.   Victoria Arch. The original arch, built in 1838, was only fifteen feet wide. It was given the name Victoria Arc
in 1898 by Gustav Friedrich Wermig, the first chairman of W.U.D.C. This picture shows the widening during 1906-0

Guildford Road. Woking.

W.H.A.3722.

37.   Guildford Road, looking towards Victoria Arch. After the death of Mr George Rastrick in 1905, the land on the right was sold, enabling these shops to be built. The buildings on the left were demolished in 1983, to make way for office development.

38.   The Technical School, Station Approach, as viewed from where Lynton House now stands. The land was sold in 1905 to Mr W.C. Slocock for £3,000, but in 1909 the County Council acquired the site to build a secondary school. It was opened in 1914 and later became the Boys' Grammar School.

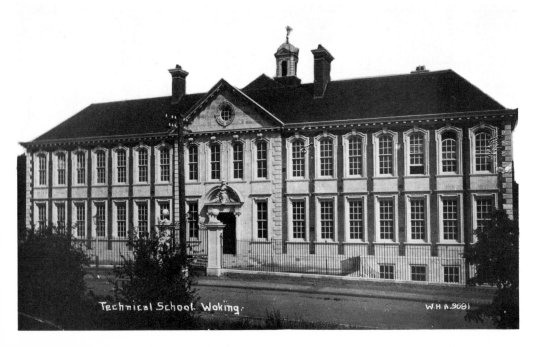

Technical School. Woking.

W.H.A.9081

9. Guildford Road, at the junction with Heathside Road and Station Approach. On the left can be seen the police station, which was opened in 1887. It contained four cells and room for three police officers. The land was bought in 1886 for £300; the building cost over £2,500.

40. Woking's Police Force, 1910. In 1871 the Woking Area was served by only six parish constables, but by 1908 the total had risen to 31, including 14 constables, 2 sergeants, an inspector and a superintendent. This photograph, taken on 7 March 1910, shows the entire Woking police force with Supt. Marks (the first superintendent in Woking) sitting in the centre of the front row. Less than one month after this photograph was taken, the strength of the Woking Division was increased to 39.

41.   Guildford Road. Opposite the police station was the *Railway Hotel*. This later became the *Cardinal* and more recently *The Sovereigns*. It was built in 1840 by Edward Woods and was the first building, other than the railway station to be built on Woking Common. In the days before a branch line was built to Portsmouth, coaches from Guildford, carrying passengers to London, would stop at the *Railway Hotel*, to allow the passengers to refresh themselves in the bar and the horses to drink from the trough on the green outside.

42.   The Corner of Guildford Road and Constitution Hill, c. 1902. At this time the large building in the centre was a private house. It later became the *Cotteridge Hotel*. The building on the right was originally the stable block.

43. The Corner of Claremont Avenue with Wych Hill Lane on the left. In 1883 the Cross Lanes Estate was sold for development to various small builders. Claremont Avenue was constructed in 1887. Its name commemorates the visit by the Duchess of Albany (who lived at Claremont, Esher) to lay the foundation stone of Christ Church.

44. The original Outdoor Swimming Pool in Woking Park was built in 1910, and constructed of wooden planks. It was only 100 feet long by 40 feet wide, with the water supplied from the nearby Hoe Stream. The present outdoor pool was built in the 1930s for £21,600.

Hill View Road, Woking.

45.   Hillview Road, c. 1910, looking from Guildford Road towards White Rose Lane. The original houses along Hillview Road were mainly built during the 1880s and 90s, but in recent years they have been replaced by modern houses and flats

46.   Heathside Road, before the houses were built and the road surface improved. The first sale of land in 1859 was not a success and it was not until after 1882 that the area began to develop as a residential district.

47. White Rose Lane, c. 1905. White Rose Lane was one of the many ancient tracks that crossed Woking Common before the railway came in 1838. It still has many twists and turns helping it keep its rural appearance. This picture shows the point where the footpath from Old Woking to Maybury crosses the lane.

WHITE ROSE LANE,
WOKING.

48. Old Woking High Street. On the left, behind the children, is the *Queen's Head* public house. Opposite is the 16th-century cottage with fields behind.

49. Graham White's Bi-Plane, Old Woking, 21 May 1910. The arrival of an aeroplane in Woking was not a common event, so when Graham White landed his Farman bi-plane at Old Woking a large crowd gathered. He had flown to Wokin from Brooklands to answer a summons at Woking Magistrates Court for speeding in his car at over 20 m.p.h.

50. Broadmead Bridge, Old Woking. The Broadmead Bridge was built in the early part of the 19th century. It was about 50 feet long and under 12 feet wide. The six spans (all of unequal lengths) were supported by timber pillars which had decayed over the years. On 15 January 1873 part of the bridge collapsed under the weight of a traction engine and threshing machine. This resulted in the loss of three lives.

51.   Pontoon Bridge over the River Wey, Old Woking. This picture, taken a few days after the accident, shows the pontoon bridge erected by engineers from Aldershot Camp. The old bridge was repaired at a cost of £120 and continued to be used for another forty-two years until the present bridge was built in 1915.

52.   The corner of Old Woking High Street and Broadmead Road, looking west.
The house on the far left, and the buildings on the right, have all been demolished. London House, opposite the *White Horse Hotel*, is now the Post Office. Next-door is the *Old Brew House*, which was built in 1718 and restored in 1983 after a fire had gutted the building.

53.   Old Woking High Street, looking towards Send Corner. On the right can be seen the forge of Mr H. Bedford. The pointed arch doorway was built in about 1895. Further along the road is the Post Office of Mr Weber and opposite can be seen the sign of the *White Hart Hotel*.

54.   The Market House, Old Woking, taken from the corner of the High Street and Church Street, c. 1895. The Market House was thought to have been built by Sir James Zouch in 1665. It was used as a corn store until about 1908 when it was replaced by a row of cottages.

55. Church Street, Old Woking taken from the corner of the High Street looking towards St Peter's church. This church was originally built in Norman times, but it was enlarged in the 13th century when the south aisle was added, and altered considerably during the last century. The building on the right remains as do the cottages nearest the church; however, many of the buildings on the left have since been replaced.

56. Pupils of Church Street School, Old Woking. Church Street School was built in 1848 as a National School supported by the Church of England Education Society. In 1876 the Woking School Board took over the responsibility of running the school and in January 1877, after improvements had been made, it was re-opened as a Board School with 35 children on its register. Further improvements were carried out between 1899 and 1901.

57. The Sewage Farm & Drainage Committee of Woking U.D.C. The building of a sewage works was one of the first tasks for the Woking Urban District Council when it was formed in 1895. Several plans were submitted and after much debate a site was chosen in Carters Lane, Old Woking. The sewage works were built between 1896 and 1899 at a total cost of £64,000.

58. Hoe Bridge, looking across the cornfields towards Old Woking village. The old bridge was built during the middle of the last century, although earlier structures have been recorded. The name 'Hoe' is supposed to derive from the Celtic 'Cors', meaning 'bog', although the Old English 'Hoh', meaning 'spur of hill', has also been suggested.

59. The London & South Western Railway Servants Orphanage, c. 1909. The L & SWRSO was founded in 1885 by Canon Allen Edwards, who, with the help of local railwaymen, set up a home for orphaned children in a rented house at Clapham, London. In 1909 a new home 'in the country' was opened at Woking, caring for 150 children. It now accommodates the elderly as well as the young.

60. L & SWRS Orphanage Boys Gymnastic Squad, c. 1915. Over the years the home was extended. In 1930 a hospital block was added and by 1932 the gymnasium was built.

61.   The London & South Western Railway
Servants Orphanage. Girls at play.

SHAH JEHAN MOSQUE, WOKING.   H.463

62.   Shah Jehan Mosque. The Mosque was built in 1889 and
named after His Highness the Shah Jehan, who was the main
benefactor. It was the first Mosque to be built in Britain and
remained the centre of Islam in this country for several years.

THE INTERIOR VIEW.
THE SHAH JEHAN MOSQUE, WOKING.

63. Interior of **Shah Jehan Mosque**. Its design, based on drawings of Mosques in India, was a problem for the architects who wrote in 1889, 'we wish the Mosque at Woking had been built at Jericho or some place distant enough never to have troubled us'. The Mosque was closed in 1899 but re-opened again in 1912.

64. Oriental Institute. The building was originally constructed as the Royal Dramatic College, a Home for retired actors and actresses. In 1884 Dr. Gottlieb Wilhelm Leitner bought the site and set up the Oriental Institute, a centre of oriental language, culture and history in Britain. The Institute led to the building of the Mosque in 1889, but when Leitner died in 1899 the Institute closed.

WOKING.—ORIENTAL INSTITUTE

65. Workmen at Martinsydes Aircraft Ltd., c. 1916. In 1910 (eleven years after the Institute closed) the Electric Accumulator Supply Company moved into part of the building. This was the first of several industries that were to occupy the site. In 1914 the partnership of Mr H.P. Martin and Mr G.H. Handasyde started making aeroplanes in the large central hall. The workforce helped produce many planes throughout the First World War, but when demand fell in 1924 the company closed. In 1926 James Walker Limited purchased the building to become the last and most successful owners of the site so far.

66. The Visit by King George V and Queen Mary to Martinsydes. On 27 April 1917 the King and Queen, accompanied by Prince Albert and Princess Mary, toured Martinsydes Aircraft Factory.

57.   Maybury Common, c. 1901. This picture shows a footpath across Maybury Common linking Old Woking Road and Monument Road. The scene today would show the former Girls Grammar School on the left, with the footpath replaced by East Hill Road.

58.   Return from Summer Camp, c. 1908. This picture, taken on the Old Woking Road near the foot of East Hill, shows a group of children returning from a camping expedition at Newark Priory. The picture has been preserved by Mr T. Fuller, whose father can be seen helping to pull the cart laden with equipment.

Back View of St. Martin's Home, Pyrford.

69.   St. Martin's & St. Nicholas's Home. The Church of England Waifs and Strays
Society's Home, originally in Pyrford Road, West Byfleet, moved in 1906 to St.
Nicholas's Home at Pyrford. In 1915 the adjoining house of St. Martin's was erected.
In 1918 Mr Rowley Bristow began work in the hospital, treating and curing the Home's
children. When he died in 1947 the hospital was renamed to his memory.

70.   A Class of Children at Pyrford School, at the turn of the century. Pyrford was the first village in the area to
have a National School. It was built in 1847 with 32 places. A new school on the corner of Coldharbour Road and
Engliff Lane was opened in 1893 with an extra 30 places. It was enlarged in 1909.

71.   The Pyrford Stone, on the corner of Upshot Lane, Pyrford Common Road, and Church Hill. The Pyrford Stone, believed to be of prehistoric origin, stood at the junction of these three lanes until 1976 when it was removed because of road improvements. It now stands on the green at the entrance to Pyrford Court, a few yards from its original position.

72.   Church Hill, Pyrford. On the right is Church Farm, whilst in the background, partly hidden by its cedar tree, is St Nicholas' Church. The church was built in the 12th century on the ridge overlooking the Wey valley. The church is perhaps most famous for its 12th- and 13th - century wall paintings which were discovered during restoration work in the last century.

73.   Plough Bridge, Byfleet. This picture, taken before the bridge was rebuilt in 1903-04, shows the main road through Byfleet to Weybridge with St. George's Hill in the background.

74.   View from Plough Bridge, Byfleet. The area around Byfleet was very prone to flooding. In February 1900 the water rose higher than it had done for over 75 years, making the Plough Bridge impassable for several days.

75. Brooklands Motor Track, although now within Weybridge, was originally part of the parish of Byfleet. It was built by Mr H.F. Locke-King on land formerly belonging to Wintersells and Brooklands Farms. Work began in the autumn of 1906 and was finished by the spring of 1907. The track was made of concrete, laid to a depth of six or seven inches. It was 100 feet wide and, in places, over 30 feet high. This allowed cars to travel at much higher speeds than had previously been possible.

76. The entrance to Brooklands Race Track, May 1908, with Inspector Mathews on traffic control duty.

Flying at Brooklands, Weybridge.

A.S. No. 11

77.   Flying at Brooklands. In addition to a motor track, Brooklands also provided an airfield for some of the earliest flying machines. Aviators such as A.V. Roe, N.S. Percival, and T.O.M. Sopwith all flew at Brooklands, and the area soon became a centre of aircraft production which has continued to this day.

78.   The Clock House, Byfleet, on the corner of Church Road and High Road. This impressive building used to be known as Byfleet Lodge and was built in the mid 19th century. It is now an old people's home.

The Clock House, Byfleet.

BLUE ANCHOR HOTEL, BYFLEET.

79.   Blue Anchor Hotel, High Road, Byfleet. The licensee, Mr Alfred Jones, was murdered here on the 29th March 1924. Whilst on holiday in France, Mrs Jones met Jean Pierre Vaquier and by the end of the holiday they were living together. When she returned to Byfleet, Vaquier followed, eventually staying at the *Blue Anchor*. A party was held at the *Blue Anchor* on 28 March. The following morning Mr Jones went downstairs to take some bromo salts. He died shortly after from strychnine poisoning. Despite Vaquier's attempt to destroy the evidence, traces of the deadly poison were found and it was later discovered that a few weeks earlier he had purchased 0.12 grammes of strychnine from a chemist in London. Vaquier was later charged and convicted of the murder.

80.   High Road, Byfleet, looking towards the Blue Anchor Hotel. The pony and cart of C. Digby (grocer) can be seen outside the shop.

HIGH RD BYFLEET

81.   High Road, Byfleet. On the right can be seen Arkells, the Byfleet Drapery Bazaar. Next to that is the Binfield bakery, with the building of the Sanway Laundry opposite.

82.   Byfleet Parish Hall. The Parish Hall was built to commemorate the Diamond Jubilee of Queen Victoria. At a meeting, held in May 1897, Mr F.C. Stoop of West Hall offered to build a village hall and club house, providing the par could find a suitable site and furnish the building. Mr H.F. Locke-King gave the site and work began in May 1898. The Parish Hall was opened in December 1898 by Lady Louisa Egerton.

83. Byfleet Church School, c. 1919. This picture shows three pupils at the Byfleet Church School. They are from left to right Miss D. Bowey, Miss A. Bird and Miss L. Vausden. They were given the honour of carrying the banner, as they had knitted the most articles for the troops during the First World War.

84. Byfleet Church. St. Mary's Church, Byfleet, was originally built in the 14th century, but has many later additions. In 1841 the south aisle was added and in 1868 the tower was restored for £210.

85. St. Mary's Church, Byfleet, on the corner of Church Road and Sanway Road. Like many other churches in the area, St. Mary's was built away from the village centre, but in recent years the surrounding fields have been replaced by housing estates and the lane has lost its rural appearance.

86. The Byfleet Fire Brigade, c. 1932. There had been a volunteer fire brigade since the mid 1880s run by Sir James Whitticker-Ellis. In 1894 the Byfleet Parish Council took over control and in 1896 they moved to the newly constructed fire station in High Road. The brigade originally only had a manual engine, but in April 1908 a steam powered engine was bought, the cost being paid for from voluntary contributions. In 1923 a motor engine was purchased by the Parish Council for £1,780.

7.   Parvis Bridge and Boathouse, Byfleet.   The Wey Navigation divided the parish of Byfleet, separating the village
om the commonland around Byfleet Corner. Dartnell's Wood was enclosed in 1806, and between 1884 and 1898 it
as divided up for sale. Amongst the attractions of the Dartnell Park Estate were the tennis club and boat house for
e exclusive use of the residents.

8.   Camphill Road looking towards Byfleet Corner with St. John the Baptist's church on the left. Its foundation stone
as laid by Mrs F.C. Stoop in 1910, and the church was opened in June 1912 at a cost of £12,000. Before St. John the
aptist was built, an iron hut at Broadoaks was used for services.

89.   Byfleet Corner. The junction of Camphill Road, Old Woking Road and Pyrford Road was always known as Byfleet Corner. It was mainly wasteland until 1887 when the London & South Western Railway Co. built a station between Camphill Road and Sheerwater Road to serve the communities of Byfleet, Pyrford and Woodham. Muggleton's shop can be seen on the left, and Barclay's Bank is on the corner of Pyrford Road.

90.   Byfleet Corner, with the church in the background.

91.   Rosemount Terrace, West Byfleet, c. 1933. Most of the land around Byfleet & Woodham Station (later renamed West Byfleet) was sold between 1881 and 1914. As the population grew, some of the larger houses (which had only been built a few years earlier) were pulled down to make way for new houses and shops. Rosemount Terrace was built on part of the grounds of Rosemount House in 1906 and 1907.

92.   Station Approach, West Byfleet, c. 1899, looking from Old Woking Road towards Madeira Road and the station. The newly constructed houses on the left of this picture have now been replaced by West Byfleet Health Centre and car park. On the right was the Sheer House Hotel which was demolished to make way for an office block and shops.

93.   Madeira Road, West Byfleet. Madeira Road has changed considerably since this picture was taken. Most of the large houses and grounds have been replaced by modern flats and houses.

94.   Sheerwater Road, West Byfleet, looking from Sheerwater towards West Byfleet. Unfortunately, the house on the right (at the corner of Old Avenue) no longer has a thatched roof, and many of the trees that once lined both sides of the road have disappeared.

95. Old Avenue, West Byfleet. Old Avenue was laid out in the late 1920s on land formerly belonging to Sheerwater Farm. It was developed as a high class residential area, being shaded from the railway to the south by trees, and having open ground to the north. This ground later became part of the G.L.C's Sheerwater Estate, built during the 1940s and 50s.

6. Byfleet Hotel, West Byfleet. The original *Byfleet Hotel* on the corner of Claremont Road and Station Road appears to have been called at one time the *Station Hotel.* The old name can be seen on the white board on the side of the building. Some of the houses in Birchwood Road can be seen in the background across the open land now occupied by the houses of Station Road.

97.   Station Road, West Byfleet. Most of the buildings in this picture have remained unchanged. The main difference is the condition of the road and paths.

Birch Walk, West Byfleet.   AS. No. 711.

98.   Birch Walk, West Byfleet. This footpath from West Byfleet Station over the Basingstoke canal to Woodham Lane has always been a favourite place for Sunday walks.

9.   Lock Three of the Woodham flight of locks on the Basingstoke canal at West Byfleet. The main part of the house
*side the lock still remains, although the single storey building has been rebuilt.

*0. Woodham Cross Road's. Woodham crossroads have changed considerably over the years. At first there were only
*e roads meeting on the common, but later Woodham Road was added. The junction then came to be known by its
*esent name 'the Six Cross Roads'. A roundabout was constructed during the 1960s.

Woodham Cross Roads, Woking

101. Woodham Church, c. 1901. All Saints Church, Woodham, was built on land donated by Mr Locke-King. Its foundation stone was laid on 11 October 1893 and less than seven months later, on 7 May 1894, the church was opened. The spire was not added until 1906 when the nave was enlarged and the chancel, chapel and vestry built.

102. Woodham Hall, c. 1901. Woodham Hall and its 67 acres of ground were sold in 1932 for housing development. Three roads called The Ridings, The Gateway and Woodham Waye were laid out. The hall was later demolished.

13. The Basingstoke Canal, with the Victoria Cottage Hospital and Wheatsheaf Bridge in the background. On the left Horsell Moor, whilst on the right can be seen some punts moored outside Beltons Boatyard along Boundary Lane.

14. Beltons Boatyard, on the Basingstoke Canal.

105. Step Bridge. Although the canal was a place of recreation, with boating, fishing and walking along the towpath, the canal was also a place of work. When it is restored, it will never be able to recapture the trade it lost to the railways and roads. Pleasure craft will replace the barges laiden with timber outside Brewster's yard.

106. Arthurs Bridge, Goldsworth. This picture shows the condition of the brickwork during the early 1920s. There is a large crack to the left of the arch and many bricks have crumbled away at its base on the right.

07. Brewery Road looking towards the junction of Church Hill and Arthurs Bridge Road, Horsell. This road gets its name from the brewery that once operated here from the mid 19th century up to the First World War. It was run by John Stedman, who claimed to produce 'beer of the highest quality from hops and barley grown locally'.

108. Church Hill, Horsell. St. Mary's Church dates from the 14th century although the south aisle (the side of which can be seen here) was built in the 15th century. The church was enlarged during the early part of this century when the north aisle, baptistry and a chapel were added. The tower was also repaired.

Horsell Schools, Woking.

S.E.Steer's Photo Series. 1503

109. Horsell C. of E. School, Church Hill. There had been a school in Horsell, run by the Baptist Church, since the late 18th century. The Church of England also had a small school in the village at this time which was enlarged in the early 19th century, and adopted as a National School in 1851. The main school buildings have changed little over the years.

110. Vicarage Lane, now Wilson Way, looking towards Horsell High Street and Church Hill. The land in the foreground is now part of the graveyard with the Vicarage garden behind. Bungalows and houses have been built on the right. This view shows how rural parts of Horsell were at the turn of the century.

111. High Street, Horsell looking from opposite the Crown public house towards Church Hill. On the left is the *Red Lion Hotel*, which at one time sold roses grown in local nurseries. The roof of the village school can be seen on the right.

112. Horsell High Street. On the left can be seen the Parish Hall, which was built in 1907. On the right is the 18th-century building that was once Horsell's Post Office. The sign for the Crown Inn is visible beyond this building with the Red Lion Hotel in the background.

High St. & Parish Hall, Horsell, Woking.

S.E. Steers
Photo Series No. 162.

113. Horsell High Street with another of Horsell's Post Offices on the right. This is now Benstead's Garage.

114. Bury Lane, Horsell, looking from the corner of Ormonde Road towards Manor Road. This section of Bury Lane has changed little over the years. It is still very narrow, with no footpath on the right hand side.

15. Manor Road, Horsell. Only the houses on the left remain. The Evangelical Church on the right was demolished in September 1983. The land in the foreground has now been built on and the road made up, the costs being shared by the local residents in the early 1930s.

116. Waldens Park Road, from the corner of Kirby Road looking towards Well Lane roundabout. The large detached houses of Waldens Park Road were begun in 1898. The village was increasing in size quite rapidly during this period as the land of Abbey Farm, Waldens Farm and some of the small Nurseries were sold for housing development.

117. Russell Road, Horsell. This picture, taken from the corner of South Road, shows workmen in the process of repairing and resurfacing Russell Road. The road was originally constructed between 1902 and 1904 when the small estate of villas and cottages were sold under the title of 'The Horsell Common Estate'.

118. Russell Road, Horsell.
The result of the work can be seen
in this picture taken from a similar
position.

119. Robin Hood Road, Knaphill,
looking towards the foot of Anchor
Hill, with the *Royal Oak* public
house in the background. This small
single storey thatched building, on
the left of Robin Hood Road, was
the local blacksmith's forge at the
turn of the century. Unfortunately
the building has long since
disappeared.

120. Robin Hood Road, Knaphill.
Opposite the forge was another old
thatched building. This was the
coffin maker's workshop. The small
door, next to the man on the left,
was specially constructed at waist
height to allow the coffins to be
removed from the workshop and
loaded onto the carts.

121. Anchor Hill, Knaphill, looking down the hill from the corner of Barley Mow Lane. The land on the left is now occupied by shops and houses. The sign on the side of the house to the right reads 'C. Bowring Carpenter & Joiner'.

122. Knaphill High Street, from the corner with the Broadway looking towards Anchor Hill. On the left is the shop of F. Belcher (at one time the village post office) whilst William Rugly's 'Newsagents, Drapers and Milliners' is on the right. The building next to Rugly's has also been a post office, but is now replaced by the Co-op supermarket.

123. High Street, Knaphill, taken from the site of the present Co-operative Store, looking towards the corner of the Broadway and the High Street where Knaphill's first Co-operative shop was built in 1913. It was the second branch of the Woking & District Co-operative Society which began business in Woking during 1899. This small single storey building is now an estate agent's.

124. High Street, Knaphill, with the Crown public house on the right. On the left was Thomas's the chemist followed by W. Johnson the greengrocers.

125. High Street, Knaphill, looking from the corner of Sussex Road towards the village centre. All the buildings on the right, from E. Pike's shop as far as the white board, have been replaced by new houses. The land on the left has also been built on.

126. The View from Reidon Hill looking across the Common towards the junction of Limecroft Road, Chobham Road and Knaphill High Street. The house on the left can still be seen, as well as the *Garibaldi* public house on the right. New houses have been built opposite the *Garibaldi*.

127. Knaphill Church, Chobham Road, c. 1905. The picture shows the old church constructed in 1885 with the church hall on the right. The present Holy Trinity Church was built on the land between these two buildings.

28. Knaphill Church, c. 1908. The new Holy Trinity Church was begun in 1907 when the Duchess of Albany laid the foundation stone. The old church, which is just visible on the left, was later pulled down and replaced by houses.

129. Brookwood Asylum. Work started on the Surrey County Pauper Lunatic Asylum (now Brookwood Hospital) in 1863. It was opened in June 1867. A farm provided fresh food and work for some of the patients. Other sources of employment included gas and water supplies and a sewage works.

Main Blocks, Brookwood Asylum.

Published by Ruglys, Knapp Hill.

130. The Lock near Langmans (or Goldsworth) Bridge, St. John's. This picture, taken in March 1911, clearly shows the decay of the Basingstoke Canal in the early part of this century.

131. The Canal, St. John's. This view taken from Kiln Bridge shows the Basingstoke Canal's lock no. 11. The houses of Copse Road can be seen on the left. The nursery in the background is now part of the Goldsworth Park Estate.

132. Robin Hood Road, St. John's, looking south, with the fields and out-buildings of Brookwood Farm on the left. In the distance can be seen the rooftops of St. John's village.

133. St. John's Church. St. John's, the Baptist Church, was built in 1840 as a Chapel of Ease to the Parish of St. Peter's, Old Woking. It was originally designed by George Gilbert Scott but has had many later additions. In 1884 St. John's Parish was formed, covering the area from Maybury in the east to Brookwood in the west.

134. St. John's Road, looking towards Kiln Bridge from the junction of St. John's Hill Road. On the left is the shop of T. Hizzey & Son. There were only a few cottages in the area prior to the 1860s, centred on Kiln Bridge and the brick making industry. During the next two decades the area started to develop quite rapidly, due mainly to the building of the convict prison and lunatic asylum.

135. St. John's Post Office, c. 1908. The actual building has changed little over the years, although its surroundings have altered. This postcard was published by H.K. Jolliffe, who ran the Post Office at that time.

136. Woking Crematorium, St. John's. In 1879 the Cremation Society of England built the first crematorium in this country at St. John's. It remained unused for six years, as the law regarding cremation was uncertain. In 1884 a famous court case in Wales ruled that cremation was in fact legal, provided that 'No nuisance was caused'. Woking's first cremation took place on 26 March 1885. The practice, however, was not very popular until after the First World War.

INKERMAN BARRACKS. PRINCIPAL ENTRANCE

137. Main Entrance, Inkerman Barracks. The ownership of part of the former convict prison was transferred from the Home Office to the War Department in 1889. The buildings were converted in 1895 and renamed Inkerman Barracks. The oldest building had been in use for less than thirty years, and the female prison which was the last to close, had only been erected in 1868. The barracks remained in use for 70 years until they finally closed in 1965.

138. Inkerman Barracks, c. 1901. The buildings dominated the landscape. The 190 ft. high Clock Tower was built in 1858 to the design of Arthur Blomfield. The west wing of the prison catered for the sick and insane, whilst the east housed those able to work. The War Department used part of this building as a military prison until 1918.

Y·M·C·A·(BARRACK SQUARE) INKERMAN BARRACKS, St.JOHN'S, WOKING.

139. The Y.M.C.A. Hut, Inkerman Barracks. Princess Victoria opened the Y.M.C.A. recreation hut at Inkerman Barracks in August 1916.

140. Hermitage Bridge, c. 1900. This picture shows the temporary wooden structure which replaced the old brick arch that was built in the 1790s.

Cross Roads, Brookwood.

W.H.A.1624

141. Brookwood Crossroads, the junction of Bagshot Road, Connaught Road and Brookwood Lye Road. This view, taken from Connaught Road, shows the houses at the crossroads, and the quiet country lane winding its way across Brookwood Lye, towards Hermitage Hill (in the background) and St. John's.

142. Brookwood Crossroads, seen from the land on the corner of Connaught Road and the road to Guildford. Stumps Bridge can be seen in the centre of the picture.

CROSS ROADS, BROOKWOOD

143. Brookwood Stumps Bridge looking towards the Crossroads. The poor condition of the road surface and bridge are well illustrated in this view taken during the early 1920s. The railway embankment can be seen in the background. Part of the canal lock is just visible to the right of the bridge.

144. The Lock at Brookwood near Stumps Bridge.
The Basingstoke Canal was a popular subject for
photographers in the early 1900s. They recorded
almost every bridge and lock, plus many places in
between. Most of the pictures of the canal below
St. John's show there was no lack of water, but this
view of Stumps Bridge Lock typifies the neglect of the
canal in this area by the early 20th century.

Canal Lock, East Brookwood. Blomfields PhotoSeries. 63

145. Connaught Road, Brookwood, c. 1905.
The land on either side of Connaught Road was still
part of the common when this photograph was taken.
The only building to be seen is the school, built in
1903 by the Woking School Board.

The Schools, Brookwood. W.H.A. 1622.

146. Station Approach, Brookwood from the corner of Connaught Road looking towards the Railway Station which was constructed in 1864. On the right can be seen the *Brookwood Hotel* built shortly after the station was opened.

147. St. Saviours Church, Connaught Road, Brookwood. Brookwood was originally part of the parish of St. Peter's, Old Woking. In 1884 it was included in the parish of St. John's, before finally becoming a separate parish when St. Saviour's Church was built in 1909.

148. Connaught Road, Brookwood. On the right is W. Mundens, 'Boot & Shoe-maker, Draper, Milliner and Hosier'. All the buildings in this picture survive, although the spire of what was the Primitive Methodist Church no longer exists. Mundens is now a fish and chip shop.

149. Connaught Road, Brookwood. All the houses in this picture remain, as do many of the Victorian and Edwardian buildings in Brookwood. Most of the modern houses in the village have been erected on the few undeveloped areas, such as the site to the left of this picture.

50. The Gamekeeper's Cottage, Brookwood. This picture of the gamekeeper's cottage at Brookwood is a reminder of ᴛe days when the 'Brook - Wood' was a royal hunting ground. Because of its isolation, this area was very popular with ᴏachers.

51. North Station. Brookwood Cemetery looking towards the Cemetery Pales and South Station. In 1854 the London ᴎecropolis & National Mausoleum Company constructed a railway branch line from Brookwood junction. This enabled ᴜneral parties to travel from the Company's station near Waterloo to the cemetery. Both stations had refreshment bars ᴎd chapels nearby. Unfortunately the stations no longer exist and most of the chapels are in need of repair. The Russian ᴏrthodox Church, however, have recently renovated the chapel at the south station.

152. Triggs Lock, Sutton Green.
Building the Wey Navigation was
the idea of Sir Richard Weston
(grandson of the builder of Sutton
Place). Work began in 1651 and by
the time Sir Richard died in May
1652, ten miles had been dug. The
original estimate for construction
was £6,000, but prices increased
causing the Weston family to fall
into debt. By the time the
Navigation was opened in 1653, it
had cost £10,000. When completed
it proved highly profitable,
especially when the Wey and Arun
Canal was opened in 1816, linking
London with the South Coast.

Worplesdon. Burden Shot, Hill.

153. Burdenshot Hill at the junction of Prey Heath Lane and Smarts Heath Lane.

154. The Owen Stone Works, Worplesdon Station, taken from the station looking towards Guildford, c. 1899. The Owen Stone Co. Ltd. started producing artificial stone in 1895. It was made from local sand and other materials. After being subjected to severe tests which included heat, cold, fire and crushing, the *British Architects Magazine* described the stone as being 'equal to the best Portland.' They were soon proved wrong. It was found that the stone quickly crumbled after only a few years. The company closed in 1908.

155. Erecting the Chimney, Owen Stone Works. This picture shows a group of over 30 workmen erecting the large 60 ft. high chimney at the works in 1895.

156. The Mayford Arms, c. 1897. During the summer, carriages were often hired to carry parties on day trips to Hind
or Newlands Corner. This picture shows two carriages outside the old *Mayford Arms*. Mr Vernon Robinson, the propr
of the public house, can be seen in the driving seat of the first carriage. The building in this picture was converted into
private house in 1905 when the present *Mayford Arms* was built.

157. Egley Road taken from the junction of Guildford Road and Smarts Heath Road. On the right can be seen Hunts Farm which was built in the 16th century. The *Bird In Hand* public house is just visible in the background.

158. The *Bird in Hand*, on the edge of Mayford Green, was built in the 1880s when the house to the left of the picture was also constructed. The Egley Road to Woking can be seen on the right.

159. Smarts Heath Road looking towards the junction of Guildford Road and Egley Road. On the left is the Mayford Stores, built in the early 19th century. Mayford was first mentioned in 1210-12, but its situation and name suggest that a settlement existed here during Anglo-Saxon times. The ford through the Hoe stream was the focus of the main roads from Guildford to Chertsey and from Woking to Farnham.

160. The Mayford Industrial School was opened in August 1887 after moving from Byfleet Corner, where a school for the education of destitute boys not convicted of crime had been operating since 1871. The school is now known as Kinton.

161. Emmanuel Mission Hall, Saunders Lane. The Emmanuel Chapel was built in 1905 on land provided by Mrs Hervey. Before this, services were held in a ruined barn further along Saunders Lane. The new building cost £233 8s 1d to construct and was opened on 4 October 1905.

162. The Golf Club, Hook Heath. On 24 May 1892 a meeting was held in London to discuss the formation of a golf club. They wanted to find land 'that can be reached in less than an hour from London and which is subject to no rights of common'. Their requirements were soon met at Hook Heath and the Woking Golf Club was formed the following year.

Hook Heath Road, Woking.   6.C.

163. Hook Heath Road. The golf course was important to the development of Hook Heath as a residential area. In 1914 a local firm of estate agents wrote 'Golf has played no small part in the development of Woking — evidence of which is shown by the large number of choice properties built around the five excellent golf courses, which surround the town'. I was between 1895 and 1914 that most of the development of Hook Heath took place, with many houses having at least one acre of ground.

164. Star Hill looking from Hook Heath towards Wych Hill Lane. The post office and shops can be seen on the left han side of the road.

165. Triggs Lane looking towards Goldsworth Road. This picture, taken in the early 1920s, shows the widening of the road from 18 to 30 ft. The railway embankment and arch can be seen in the background.

166. The Triangle (or Slococks Corner) at the junction of Triggs Lane, St. John's Road, Goldsworth Road and the Kingsway. A roundabout has now been constructed here. Walter Slococks Nursery to the right is now part of the Goldsworth Park Estate.

167. York Road looking towards Guildford Road. York Road was built during the late 19th and early 20th century. It was named York Road to commemorate the marriage of the Duke and Duchess of York (later to become King George V and Queen Mary). Most of the buildings in this picture survive.

168. Wych Hill Lane. On the left can be seen the corner of Mount Hermon Road.

WOKING.—MOUNT HERMON ROAD

169. Mount Hermon Road with the corner of West Hill Road on the right. c. 1901. The plot of land on the left was owned by the Rev. W.F.T. Hamilton who was vicar of Christ Church, Woking, between 1893 and 1905. St. Mary of Bethany Church was built here in 1907.

170. Woking Football Club, 1908. The club won the West Surrey League in 1896, 1898, 1905 and 1908. The Surrey Charity Shield was won in 1904, 1907 and 1908; they were also runners up in 1905. The club also managed to become one of the last sixty-four teams in the F.A. Cup in 1908, but they were defeated on 11 January by the famous Bolton Wanderers.